Printed By Createspace, An Amazon.com Company

Made in United States
Orlando, FL
21 September 2023

37144256R00076